Now I Know

Story of Dinosaurs

Written by David Eastman

Illustrated by Joel Snyder

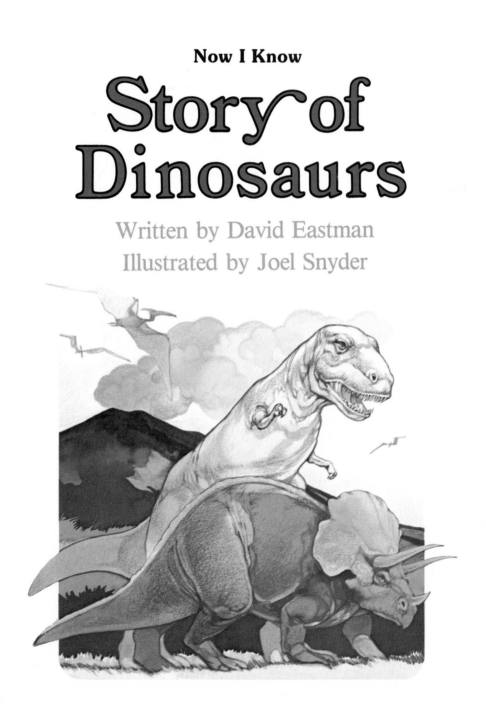

Troll Associates

Pronunciation Guide

Brachiosaurus	(Brak-ee-uh-SAWR-us)
Brontosaurus	(Bron-tuh-SAWR-us)
Diplodocus	(Dih-PLAH-duh-kuss)
Tyrannosaurus Rex	(Tie-ran-uh-SAWR-us Rex)

Library of Congress Cataloging in Publication Data

Eastman, David.
    Story of dinosaurs.

    (Now I know)
    Summary: A brief introduction to dinosaurs:
what they looked like and when and how they lived.
    1. Dinosaurs—Juvenile literature. [1. Dino-
saurs] I. Snyder, Joel, ill. II. Title.
QE862.D5E18   567.9′1   81-11363
ISBN 0-89375-648-2   AACR2
ISBN 0-89375-649-0 (pbk.)

10   9   8   7   6   5   4   3   2   1

Dinosaurs lived a long time ago.

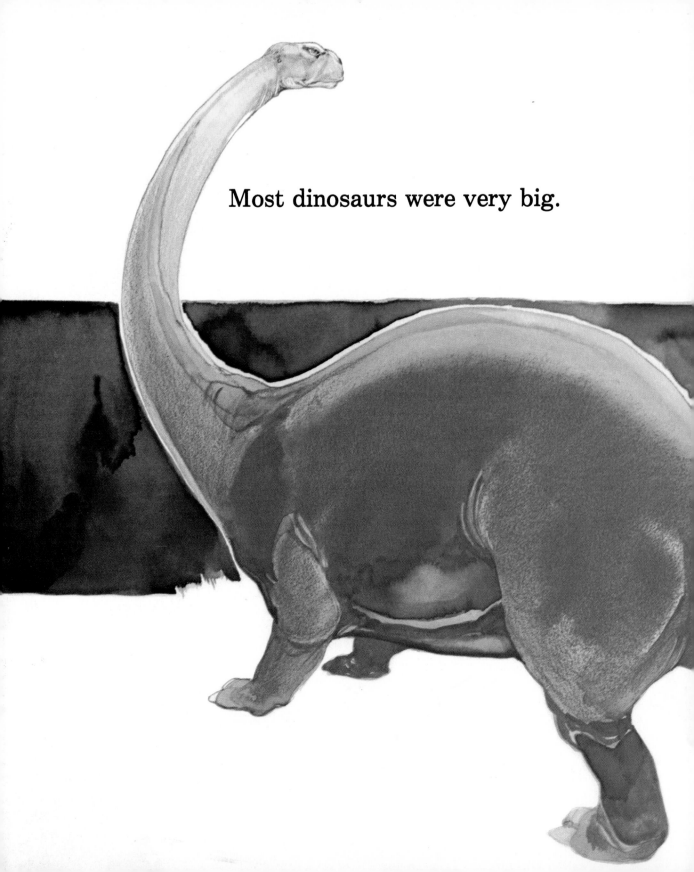

Most dinosaurs were very big.

There were many kinds of dinosaurs.

No one ever saw a
living dinosaur.

But we have found their bones.

And the bones tell us about the dinosaurs.

Tyrannosaurus Rex was
the King of the Dinosaurs.
Tyrannosaurus had a big head,
and long sharp teeth.

Tyrannosaurus walked on two legs,
and liked to eat meat.

But not all dinosaurs ate meat.

Brontosaurus ate plants,
and walked on four legs.

Brachiosaurus ate plants, too.

He was the heaviest dinosaur of all.

He had a very long neck.

Some dinosaurs had sharp points on their sides...

or bony plates on their backs.

This dinosaur had a
"sail" on its back.

And this one had a bill like a duck!

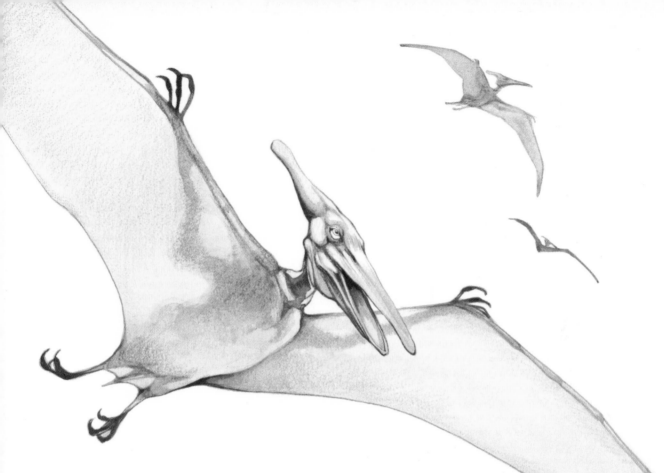

Many strange animals lived at the same time
as the dinosaurs. Some had long wings.

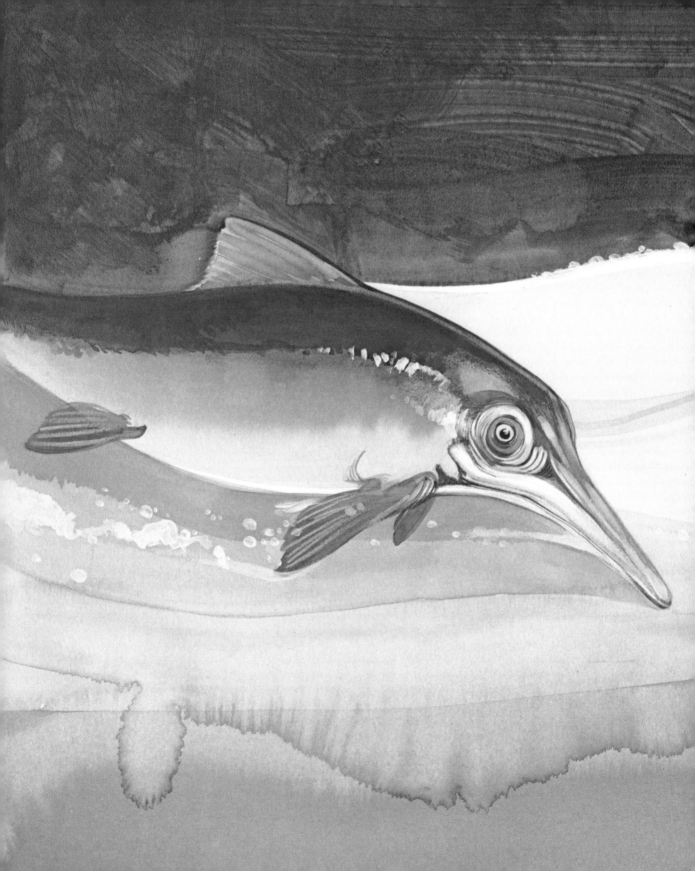

Other strange animals lived in the sea.

Some looked like fish.

Some looked like huge alligators or sea monsters.

They had flippers instead of feet.

But the dinosaurs were the
biggest animals that ever lived.

Diplodocus was as long as 10 elephants.

From head to tail, Diplodocus
was the longest dinosaur.

Dinosaurs lived a long time ago.

And—in their time—they ruled the world.

But that was long long ago.